The Narcissist Man

A Battle Between a Lie and the Light That Would Not Die

By

Allison Latoya Lewis

Declaration

I was set up and betrayed by people I once trusted with, community leaders, council workers, and those in positions of authority. They spread lies about me, slandered my name on social media, and turned people I knew against me.

Even those meant to help, including the police and my job centre advisor, were influenced by those working within the council. They worked together to discredit me, to silence me, and to make me appear unstable.

All of this began because of my faith in Jesus Christ. When they learned about my spiritual gifts, they tried to draw me into practices that went against my beliefs. When I refused to take part, they turned on me — using power, manipulation, and deceit to destroy my character and isolate me.

But I will not be silenced.

I will not bow to their lies or their control. My faith remains my shield, and my truth is my defense.

This book is my declaration — a testimony of what I have endured and the strength I've found in God's light.

Contents

Declaration i

Prologue 1

Chapter 1: The Hum of Shadows 7

Chapter 2 – Waking into Lies 14

Chapter 3 – A Marriage I Never Chose 24

Chapter 4 – The Web 31

Chapter 5 – Witchcraft in the Walls 44

Chapter 6 – An Attack on Blood 50

Chapter 7 – The Smear Campaign 60

Chapter 8 – Truth Restored 64

Prologue

I am not okay.

I am not okay.

But I'm breathing.

So maybe that's enough for now.

The walls whisper things I didn't say.

My name echoes from mouths I never met.

People are building stories using my bones.

They call it concern. They call it help.

They call it madness.

But I call it **theft**.

Someone is trying to erase me.

They want to wear my face like a mask.

Say my name like they earned it.

Live in my house like I'm the ghost.

But I'm still here.

I still bleed when I break skin.
I still blink when the light hits my eyes.

I still speak.
Even when no one listens.
Even when they try to talk over me or to bury my words beneath paperwork and lies.

He says he's my husband.
He says we're married.
He says I belong to him.

I don't belong to anyone.

I never says, "I do."
I never says, "Come in or take it all."
But he moved in anyway—
into my address,
into my name,
into my silence…

He's loud in places I never gave him permission to enter.
He walks around as if he has earned this life.
Like he bought it with something more than greed.
But all he paid with was lies.

And still, they believe him.

They believe the man in the black jacket. The man with stories stitched into his smile. The man who sends his shadow to sit outside my

window
and calls it love.

They don't hear the engine at 2 am.

They don't smell the smoke under my door. They don't see him watching.

Waiting.

I do.

I see the way he looks at my life like a prize.

I see the children I never birthed calling me Mom.

I see the council ignoring my leaking ceiling like they were told to.

I see the doctor pretending concern while drawing invisible lines on paper.

She wants me medicated.

He wants me married.

They all want me muted.

But I'm still talking.

Even if it's only to God.

He listens.

Even when I whisper.

Even when my voice is made of glass.

Even when I sob through prayers that don't rhyme.

They think I'm losing my mind.

But really, I'm losing my patience.

There's a difference.

I've been hunted by kindness disguised as knives.

Watched smiles turn into cages.

Watched concern become control.

But I won't bow.

I wasn't made in silence.

I wasn't made for easy death.

I am the wrong woman to haunt.

They call me broken.

But I call myself **refined by fire.**

The kind that doesn't burn out.

Not yet.

Not while I still remember who I am.

Not while God keeps pulling me back from the edge.

I am not okay.

But I'm awake.

And I see everything now.

The shadows that pretend to be light.

The love that smells like gasoline.

And the promises that feel like cages.

And tonight, I saw myself.

Not in a dream. Not in a vision.

In that old, long mirror standing in the corner — the one I always avoid when the house gets too quiet.

She stopped.

Not me.

She stopped.

She was made of scripture and thunder.

Her eyes didn't blink.

Her fists didn't shake.

She stared right through me.

And her lips moved.

But what she whispered… wasn't meant for this world.

And now, neither am I.

Chapter 1: The Hum of Shadows

The night has fallen, and an eerie silence has surrounded the area outside.

The kind of silence that used to make my skin crawl...

Because I know...

In the darkness, there's something lurking—something waiting for me.

And then, as it does every night, it happens.

The engine begins—like a motorcycle revving softly in the dark, not loud enough to shatter the silence, just enough to remind me it's there.

Low. Patient. A mechanical heartbeat pressing against the glass.

I check the clock. **2:04 a.m.** Same as last night. Same as the night before.

I drag myself to the window. The air in this room hasn't moved in hours. The heat clings to the walls like sweat, and the wallpaper in the corner is peeling again. I press two fingers to the glass and move the curtain an inch.

He's there.

His helmet was as dark as a closed casket. Visor blank, reflecting my thin slice of curtain like a blade glinting in the dark.

Same jacket. Same stance—perfectly still, like a mannequin someone left in the wrong story.

Only this time, he turns his head.

He looks up. Not fast. Not like someone caught watching. Like someone *meant* to be seen. Like someone *waiting* to be noticed.

I dropped the curtain and shoved my spine into the wall. The paint is cold, gritty, already peeling at the seams like skin that won't heal.

The room shrinks around me the way lungs close around smoke. My ceiling presses a palm to my forehead. The floor moves a fraction closer to my feet. The air goes heavy, wet wool on my chest.

The house keeps its secrets in damp corners. The leak in the bathroom dripped all day like a metronome marking time for my panic.

The mold has learned my name. It grew from tile to baseboard to cupboard, and today it reached the underside of my throat. I smell iron in the water. I tasted old metal in the morning. They will call it neglect. I will call it hex in plaster.

Another sound. A soft scrape along the outside wall. Not footsteps. Something else. Something deliberate.

"Not tonight," I whisper to the darkness. "Not tonight."

The scrape outside slides into silence, but another sound blooms inside my head — a voice, soft and raspy, curling under my skin.

"You're my wife..."

I jerk my head like I can shake the words loose. "No."

"We are married... darling. I'm your husband."

The poison in his tone lands under my ribs, a whisper meant to be a promise.

"You're a liar!" My voice cuts the air before I know it's left my mouth.

"You will accept it — soon you will."

Another voice. Or the same one changing masks. Each word, like smoke, pushed through a keyhole.

"Stop—stop—stop." My palms press against my ears until the room smears. My pulse drums against my hands, and even that sound turns to whispers.

He's rehearsing.

I can hear him. Holding the script too close to his face, smudging ink with greedy fingers. He wants to rewrite my story. I can almost feel his thumb licking the edge of my page, ready to turn it.

I peel my fingers away. The hum returns — steady outside the glass, steady in my bones. I edge back to the window. The curtain lifts like an eyelid, and I let it blink.

He's closer now.

Not the bike. The man. He's off the seat. One boot on the pavement, one hand on the throttle, the other hanging loose at his side, like he can't believe how easy this is.

He tilts his helmet toward the glass in a nod I refuse to return. For a second, I think he might raise a hand. He doesn't.

He turns instead, slow, theatrical, giving me the back of him like a stage curtain dropping after a bad act.

My breath catches. Something glints on his jacket.

A word, written in foil vinyl, was shining under the streetlight.

KILL.

My fingers tighten on the curtain until my knuckles go white. My legs refuse to move. My heartbeat stutters and then finds a rhythm I don't recognize.

What should I do? Should I call the police? No... they won't believe me. They'll ask *where?* when I say *he was here.* They'll write my name again in that file, adding words like *distressed* and *unstable.*

If you were standing next to me - if your shoulder pressed against mine - we could pretend to be brave together. We could breathe out slowly at the same time and fog the glass with one long cloud and write NO with our fingers on the same breath. You'd see it, wouldn't you? How fear edits the world down to verbs. **Hide. Listen. Pray.**

I whisper a line from the only book that's never lied to me.

"The Lord is my light and my salvation, whom shall I fear? The Lord is the stronghold of my life—of whom shall I be afraid?" (Psalm 27:1)

The verse feels like a lock sliding into place. Small. Quiet. But there.

I stay at the window. He stays in the street. The jacket glows silver in the dark, the word on his back pulsing like a heartbeat.

My fingers tremble once, then still. My mouth finds its shape again.

"Turn around," I say, steady now. "Tell your master I'm not afraid. The Lord is my savior."

Just then, a porch light flickers on two houses down, sudden and intrusive.

The helmet turns, visor flashing. The bike coughs once, then pulls away, swallowed by the street before the light can reach him.

I draw a deep breath, then collapse against the wall. The paint scrapes my shoulder, the chill seeps into my skin, but I don't move. The room is silent now. Empty.

The heaviness that pressed against the glass, that curled under the door, has lifted. For the first time tonight, the air feels mine again.

"In the name of the Father…" I whisper, the words trembling into the quiet. "…the Son, and the Holy Spirit."

My eyes scan the room, tracing the outlines carved by the faint spill of streetlight through sheer curtains. Shadows stretch long across the walls, bending over the furniture, pretending to be still.

But shadows don't lie. People do.

The lies started the day I opened my eyes again. Waking into a life that wasn't mine. Waking into papers I never signed, vows I never spoke, a story already rewritten with my name at the top.

I thought survival was hard when they circled my house at night. I didn't know survival was only the prologue.

My gaze drifts upward, and my breath stills.

The clock ticks steadily on the wall.

Each click louder than the last.

Each second hits like a hammer against the door of memory.

My eyes stay fixed on it, unblinking.

The memories hit hard—

the real ones.

The ones I'm going to share with you.

Chapter 2 – Waking into Lies

The burning memory of that day is still etched into me.

The day when it all started.

The first thing my ears caught was a sharp buzz—sharp and deafening…

The kind of sound that doesn't belong to the world but to the spaces between it.

It grew louder, multiplied, layered itself with others: low murmurs, footsteps, the clipped voices of men and women, the steady beep of machines marking a rhythm I didn't set.

I tried to open my eyes, but they resisted. Behind the darkness, circles of light moved—slow at first, then faster—bright shapes chasing each other like ghosts in a carousel.

There was a pulse inside my head, thudding against bone.

And beneath it, a hum. A machine breathing on my behalf.

Then — I heard a woman's voice. Soft. Practiced. Careful. Words folded themselves in cotton before reaching me.

"Can you hear me?"

My tongue scraped against dryness. I wanted to speak, but the air felt too heavy.

I nodded—or thought I did. The movement felt borrowed.

She moved closer; I could feel the warmth of her breath when she spoke again.

"You've been asleep for a while," she said. "You're safe now."

Safe.
The word echoed—hollow, too clean, too soon.

Safe from what?

Safe with whom?

I blinked again. Once. Twice. The fog begins to lift. The ceiling above me is too white, too blank—a stretched canvas of nothing.

A slow panic built behind my ribs.

Tubes slithered from my arm like translucent veins, each one carrying something out of me—or into me.

I followed the lines with my eyes until they

vanished into a machine whispering in numbers I didn't understand.

Hospital.
The thought landed heavily.

The air smelled like metal and bleach, like life scrubbed too clean to be trusted.

I opened my mouth, and a sound finally escaped — raw and small.

"Where...?"

The nurse leaned in, smiled too kindly. "Don't try to speak yet. You've been through a lot."

I wanted to ask what happened, but before I could, she straightened.

Her hand hovered near my wrist as if waiting for permission to touch.

"I'll call your husband," she said gently. "He's been waiting for you."

Husband.

The word stung sharper than the IV in my vein. I blink once more, as if the world might rearrange itself into sense.

"I'm… not… married…" I tried to speak, but my voice came out as a whisper—did she hear it? did she not? —I don't know.

Maybe she mistook me for another patient.

But she didn't flinch. Didn't question.

"Let me call him."

She only offered another practiced smile, the kind they must teach in nursing school, and slipped quietly out of the room.

The silence that followed felt heavier than the machines.

I tried to sit up, but my body feels wrong, as though someone rewired the connection between thought and motion while I slept.

The room hummed again, lights flickered like a pulse against the floor.

Footsteps returned. Slower this time.

A shadow lengthened across the door.

And he stepped inside.

Tall. Dark jacket. Hair combed like someone preparing for a photograph.

His eyes found mine, and for a moment I couldn't tell if he was relieved or waiting.

I clutched the sheet beneath me, but my hands were powerless.

His dark energy suddenly cast a shadow over the room.

He can't be here…

No - he can't be….

"Oh, thank God," he breathes, stepping closer. "You're finally awake, darling. We were so scared. But I knew you'd make it."

Darling? My blood boiled and rushed to my temples.

He moved toward the bed, fingers grazing my arm—cold, heavy, like glass pressed over skin. I flinched, but he doesn't seem to care.

"You're okay now," he murmured. "We'll go home soon."

He crawled his fingers over my skin; slow strokes meant to calm, to claim.

A surge of panic and anger shot through my veins.

"Who...are..you?" I heard my voice—barely, shakily—trying to find itself.

His lips stretched into a smile.

"You must be disoriented," he said gently, the way a teacher might speak to a child who failed a test. "The accident—it was terrible. You hit your head. Memory loss is normal."

Memory loss? No. No. I'm fine.

I remember that night—that accident.

And I remember him—standing across the street, waiting, watching.

My throat closed.

He was always there—outside my home, the bus stop—following like a shadow.

He is nothing but a bloody predator. I wanted to shout, but my voice didn't support me.

A nurse drifted back in to fix the cannula.

"You're very lucky, ma'am," she said. "Your husband never left your side."

A smile was plastered on her face when she looked at the man sitting beside me.

"Oh, how could I leave my beloved wife alone?" His voice—creepy, raspy—stung like a needle.

Wife… no—what the hell is going on here?

Just as the nurse adjusted the drip, another woman stepped in—clipboard in hand, eyes tired but direct.

"Can you confirm your name for me, Mrs. ___?"

She was already writing.

I tried to answer, but before my lips could even tremble, I heard his raspy voice again

"Mrs. Carter..." His poisonous eyes were smiling at me, at my helplessness.

"No...I'm not…

I'm not…

I think I shook my head. Maybe I said something. Maybe I didn't.

Their smiles hang there, eerie under the blinding hospital lights.

My thoughts scatter, racing toward the edge of something dark—And then the darkness takes me first.

(Present)

A drop lands on my forehead. Cold. Sudden. My eyes snap open.

The ceiling greets me in silence, cracked and breathing. The leak has spread—water tracing thin silver paths down the walls like veins.

I lie still for a moment, trying to remember where I am. The hospital fades; this room pulls me back. The floor is damp beneath the thin blanket. My skin smells faintly of metal and mold.

The man on the bike is long gone, but sometimes—when the house holds its breath—I still feel the low hum of his engine vibrating through the floorboards.

Another drop falls, catches in my hair, slides behind my ear.

The sound repeats—slow, deliberate.

Drip. Drip. Drip.

The leak has gotten worse. I told them about it. I told the council weeks ago.

They said they'd send someone.

No one ever came.

No one ever comes.

Because he controls them.

He controls everything—every name, every paper, every hand that should have helped me.

The walls close in tighter when I think of it. The air tastes sour, like damp wood and betrayal.

They want me to break.

They want to see me fold into the mold, become part of the ruin.

They want me to go mad.

But I won't.

I won't give them that.

I push myself up slowly, my palms slipping against the wet floor. My limbs ache from sleep that doesn't rest. I crawl toward the dry corner near the window. Moonlight cuts through the curtains, faint and fractured, enough to turn the dust into stars.

"Just a little more rest…" I whisper to no one.

My body obeys before my mind can protest. My eyes flutter, heavy with exhaustion.

And when they close, the darkness moves—and the memories start again, rolling like a film that refuses to stop playing.

Chapter 3 – A Marriage I Never Chose

"What would you do if you fell asleep as yourself and woke up as someone else?"

That's not a riddle.

It's not the beginning of a story.

It's my reality.

The day I woke from the coma, I didn't lose my memory or my limbs.

I lost my life.

Piece by piece, signature by signature, they rewrote me into someone else's wife.

And I couldn't stop it.

Because the world around me adjusted to his lie and rejected my truth.

They believed the papers he brought — the marriage certificate, the signatures that weren't mine.
They believed the man who smiled and said I was his to protect.

To the nurse, I was his grieving wife.

To the doctor, I was a fragile woman confused after trauma.

He said I forgot things, that I made things up. And they believed him — because his lies wore suits and smiles, and mine wore exhaustion and shaking hands.

Everywhere I turned, his version followed me. Neighbors waved to him like a devoted husband. The housing officer called him "such a caring man." Even the doctor nodded when he spoke for me.

When I tried to correct them, their voices softened. "She's been through trauma," they'd whisper. "She doesn't remember."

But I do remember.

The rain that night. The crash. The man standing at the corner watching, the man who wants me dead, and the same man who now claimed to be my husband.

He walked beside me like an echo I couldn't escape, holding papers that said we shared a home, a life, a story.

Everywhere I went, he was already there — rewriting my world before I could speak it back into truth.

He moved into my house without permission, like a shadow slipping under the door. He filled it with his presence, his scent, his name—until even the walls began to forget me.

The kitchen where I made tea in silence. The couch where I once prayed. Now they all feel watched. Owned. Branded with someone else's claim.

You know it's not the violence that breaks you. It's the disbelief — the slow suffocation of people who look at you kindly while erasing your reality.

I used to believe truth could stand on its own. Now I know it can be stamped, filed, and believed by everyone except the one who lived it.

But I couldn't give up.

I decided to go to the Enfield Council because I still believed someone would listen.

That truth still mattered somewhere.

If nothing, I can at least get legal protection.

At the office, four faces watched me from across the table, polite and detached.

A clock ticked somewhere behind them, steady, indifferent, slicing seconds out of my hope.

I told them everything—about the man, the accident, the lies.

How I woke up in a hospital and found my name already rewritten.

How papers appeared with signatures that weren't mine.

They listened to the way people do when they've already chosen a side.

One of them—a woman with kind eyes that didn't match her tone—smiled thinly.

"You've been through a lot, Mrs. Carter," she said. "It's understandable that you're disoriented."

Mrs. Carter.

The name hit like a verdict.

"I'm not—"But another council member lifted a hand, cutting through my words.

"Let's not agitate ourselves. You're safe now. He's doing his best to support you. We've spoken to him."

Of course, they had.

He'd been there before me — with that poisonous smile, with stories, with proof.

He always arrived first, shaping the world to fit his lie.

I wanted to scream, *he's lying*, but the air between us was too thick with civility.

Their eyes slid over me—calculating, sympathetic, distant.
One took notes; another nodded slowly, as if I were performing grief rather than telling the truth.

When I finally stood, my voice shaking, one of them murmured, "Maybe it's time to seek help, for your peace of mind."

Peace of mind.

Their favorite phrase.

It means silence. It means compliance.

It means pretending the lie is easier to live with than the fight to undo it.

When I stepped out, he was already waiting for me outside the building.

That was a sign: You can't run.

Leaning against his car, tie loosened, confidence intact.
When our eyes met, he smiled—gentle, deliberate.

"How did it go, love?"

I said nothing.

Words were useless now; he'd already spoken for me.

He moved closer, close enough that I could smell his cologne, sharp and heavy.

"Did you tell them everything?" he asked softly. "Every little detail?"

Then, without waiting for an answer, he brushed imaginary dust off my sleeve.

"Good girl. We don't want misunderstandings."

Good girl.

The phrase scraped down my spine.

He walked me to the car as if escorting something fragile. I kept my eyes on the ground, afraid that if I looked at him too long, he'd steal whatever pieces of myself were left.

In the car, the silence thickened again.

The city outside looked unfamiliar—each building, each street sign, somehow rewritten, like the world had joined his script.

When we stopped at a light, I saw a reflection in the window. My face, pale and tired, stared back at me beside his. Two people who looked like they belonged together.

A picture-perfect lie.

That night, I tore every letter that carried his last name.
I tried to wash it off the mailbox, off the documents, off the space where my name used to live.

But ink stains deeper than blood.

And lies, once believed, don't wash off easily.

I pressed my palms together, whispering words I barely remembered:

"The Lord is my strength and my shield; my heart trusts in Him."

My voice shook, but the prayer steadied the air.

Because I knew this wasn't over. He'd built the walls high, but I could still see the cracks. And one day, I promised myself, I'd make the truth loud enough to break through them.

Chapter 4 – The Web

Psalm 12:2–3 (NIV):

"*Everyone lies to their neighbor; they flatter with their lips but harbor deception in their hearts. May the Lord silence all flattering lips and every boastful tongue...*"

My life became a living hell.

And I was watching myself getting slowly consumed by the fire.

Because the predator I was facing had no boundaries. He wasn't just trying to be in my life — He was trying to be *me*.

He would do anything to link his name with mine. Anything to make it seem like I belonged to him.

And I — trapped in this nightmare — was still trying to prove that I didn't.

He wanted my name.

My home.

My story.

And every day, I watched him inch closer to owning it all.

First, he claimed my name, my life, my house—tried to convince me that I was married. And not only married, but also that I was the mother to his kids.

Yes. This low-life person even used his children, made them call me *mom*,

And when I refused to respond, he said I had forgotten

But how could I have forgotten getting married? How could I have children I had never even met?

I only had one child—My son.

One heartbeat I carried inside me. One soul I raised with my own hands.

Those children were not mine.

And still, they sat in my kitchen. They played with my things and constantly tried to mess with my memories.

My house no longer felt like mine. He was there when I woke up. He visited uninvited. He knew which cupboard held the mugs. He moved through the hallway like someone who belonged. He claimed I had let him in, given him keys.

And when I said no—when I said I never would—he would politely say "Oh, poor baby—looks like your little brain's all scrambled"

But I remember everything.

I remember the chill of the floor when I locked myself in the bathroom just to escape him.

I remember praying against the walls, asking God to make my house feel like a home again.

But it never did.

I remember screaming under my own roof, begging for help—but I didn't know where to go.

Every time I turned to someone for help, he was already there explaining that I was unwell and suffering from memory loss.

He made madness sound like compassion.

The council listened to him. The doctor wrote notes. The neighbors nodded.

Piece by piece, their faith in him became disbelief in me.

I began receiving documents I had never signed. Housing reviews. Welfare assessments. Medical referrals. All under his name. All under *our* name.

They weren't just errors — they were erasures. Every line rewritten to exclude me. Every file was stamped with his version of who I was.

I was being rewritten — not just in the eyes of people, but in the records that governed my life.

And yet, my resistance made things very difficult for him. I refused to play along, to surrender. So, he decided to deal with me differently.

It was the 24th of the month when the phone rang.

My Job Centre advisor greeted me with her usual sugary tone, the kind people use when they're trying to hide something behind politeness. After a few questions about my payments, she changed her voice — softer, lower.

"I want to refer you to someone," she said. "From the mental health team."

I paused, confused. "Why would I need that?"

"No reason," she replied quickly. "I know you're fine — I do — but sometimes, speaking to someone can help access more support. Financially, too."

"I don't need mental health help," I told her plainly.

She laughed nervously. "I know, I know. But it might get you a bit more money. It's just a conversation."

"No," I said again, sharper this time. "I don't want that money. And I'm not speaking to anyone."

"But it's okay—"

"No, it's *not* okay," I snapped, cutting the call before she could say anything more.

A few days later, another knock at the door.

It was a woman I didn't recognize, though the narcissist man had once introduced her as an "old friend." She spoke like someone who knew me well — warm, overly familiar, slipping my name into every sentence like she was reminding me of a history we didn't share.

I said nothing. I didn't offer tea. I barely nodded.

She wasn't here for conversation. She was here for persuasion.

"There's a doctor I know," she said after a while. "A really good psychiatrist. Very gentle. He helped *me* when I was going through something difficult. You should see him."

"I don't need a psychiatrist," I said flatly.

"But it's just a chat—"

I stood up. "You want to help someone with delusions?" I pointed toward the other room. "Go speak to *them*—not me."

She left not long after that. I didn't watch her go.

That night, I sat by the window, trying to calm the chaos building in my chest. My breath came unevenly, my thoughts crowding. I closed my eyes and whispered beneath my breath — not just words, but pleas.

I asked God to show me what I was missing. To open my eyes wider. To strengthen my spirit, where the world was trying to bend it.

And then it happened.

My housing officer came the very next day — clipboard tucked under her arm, her voice low and sympathetic.

"I'm sorry for everything you're going through," she said as soon as I opened the door. "I've read your messages. I know how hard this must be."

I rushed toward her, my voice almost cracking. "Then you know the truth. You know who I am.

You *have* to help me. Please. This man is trying to erase me — he's dangerous — I need protection—"

She reached out and gently placed her hand on my arm.

"I know everything," she said. "And I promise I'm going to help you."

For a second, I believed her. My heart slowed, just slightly. Relief hovered.

"But first," she added, her voice calm, "let's get you to the doctor. Just to stabilize things. The accident was serious. You've been through a lot. Once we do that, we can figure out next steps…"

She kept speaking — her words smooth, practiced — but I wasn't listening anymore.

Because I wasn't looking at her lips.

I was looking in her eyes.

And what I saw there wasn't belief. It wasn't hope. It was pity. The same shallow, distant pity I had seen before.

That's when I knew. The damage was already done. I wasn't standing in front of help. I was standing in front of another gatekeeper — another carefully placed puppet with a script.

She didn't come to rescue me.

She came to walk me to the edge — quietly, politely — and make sure I jumped.

And in that moment, everything clicked.

The system couldn't harm that man. Because the man ran the system.

(Present)

Dong... Dong... Dong...

The sound of the hourly chime echoed through the walls like a warning.

It was 4 a.m., but outside the window, the sky still clung to night.

No moon. No stars. Just a hollow, unbroken darkness.

I was still curled into myself on the mattress, damp with the breath of the leaking ceiling, waiting — still for the morning light.

Like in the horror films where survivors hold out till dawn, believing daylight will save them.

But in my story, no light would ever be strong enough to banish the darkness I was facing.

Adam Carter – the narcissist man - wasn't just a villain in my story.

No. He was the writer, the director, and the forger of my script.

He didn't want to be near me—he wanted to *be* me.

By now, if you think this was about obsession, or some twisted infatuation—you're wrong.

It was never about love. Never about desire.

It was about control. Inheritance. Power.

He entered my life with one purpose—to erase me and take everything I was meant to have.

Me. Allison Latoya Lewis.

My name. My legacy. My house. My entire identity.

A perfect plot for a psychological thriller, maybe. But this wasn't fiction.

It was the reality I was surviving—barely.

It started with shadows. He followed me for weeks—studying me. My work routine. My movements. My relationships.

He took notes like a man preparing for a role he intended to steal.

And then came the accident.

It wasn't by chance. It was timed. Meant to end my life cleanly, convincingly.

He had already forged the documents: a marriage certificate, signatures I never gave, witnesses I never met.

Had I died that night, everything would have passed to him—just as he had planned.

But fate intervened. I survived.

And my survival ruined his perfect story.

That's why the hospital staff never questioned him. Why do you think the council nodded along? Why did even the doctors write what he whispered?

Because the lie wasn't just his, it had been carefully planted, cultivated, and *believed*.

And by the time I opened my eyes again, the world had already been rewritten around me.

I used to wonder—*was he just that convincing?* Was my voice too weak, too broken?

No. The truth was far more terrifying.

The world I woke up to was his.

It took time to see the full picture, but eventually, I did.

Many within the Enfield Council weren't just blind—they were bought. Paid. Positioned.

He didn't just build lies—he purchased them.

Marriage contracts. Council letters. Housing files. Entire systems bent around his version of reality because he had the money, the reach—and the people—to make it happen.

And he didn't act alone.

The woman who visited me—the one with the sweet voice and familiar smile, who claimed to be an old friend.

She wasn't a friend. She was *his wife*.

The same woman who gently pushed me toward a psychiatrist.
The same woman who worked—officially—for the council.

They played their roles well.

Husband and wife, dressed as saviors. Their hands stitching lies, their mouths feed doubt.

Together, they wove a web so intricate, so seamless, that anyone who stepped near me got caught in it.

They didn't just want me erased.

They wanted me silenced. Discredited. Unseen.

Dead—or worse.

Crazy.

My housing officer stopped taking my calls after that.
She refused to work for me — because I had ruined her perfect plan.

Her idea had been simple: send me to the psychiatrist, let them write *paranoid* beside my name, and the rest would unfold easily.

Once I was labeled unstable, they could take everything — my home, my story, my life.

She was never on my side.

She was on *his* payroll.

They all were.

But I crushed their plans — one after another — in the name of God.

Every time they plotted my fall, He gave me the strength to stand.

When they tried to silence me, He gave me words. When they tried to cage me in their lies, He opened a door they didn't know existed.

And when I felt unseen, He reminded me that His eyes never left me — not for a moment.

Because the truth is not written by men who forge papers.
It is written by the hand of God, and His ink does not fade.

So no matter how many versions of me they've tried to create on paper —No matter how many signatures they've forged, how many words they've twisted, how many truths they've buried —

I am still here.

And I won't let them win.

My name is still mine.

My story is still mine.

And as long as I can still speak it, they haven't won.

Chapter 5 – Witchcraft in the Walls

(Present)

The clock strikes 4:30.

The chime echoes once... then again... a slow, hollow note that wraps itself around the room like a whisper I'm not meant to hear.

Why isn't time moving?

It feels like the night has swallowed the seconds whole, trapping me in the folds of an hour that refuses to end.

A restlessness stirs in my chest — not panic, not fear... something deeper. Like my soul itself is trying to shift out of place.

And then — that sound. The one I've been hearing for weeks.

A low, unnatural hum. Not from the street. Not from the house above.

It seeps from inside the walls.

I clutch my blanket tightly around me, but it offers no warmth.

Only the sense that I'm still awake... and still alone.

Then, another sound.

At first, a soft creaking — like an old breath pressing through plaster. Then sharper. Louder.

Like something crawling just above the ceiling tiles... slow... intentional... as if it knows I'm listening.

Water drips again. But this time, not from the usual corner.
This drop comes from a different wall — a clean wall. A wall that's been dry for weeks.

I turn toward it.

A thin line of water snakes down the paint, carving its own path.

The smell follows — mold, but sweet. Too sweet. Like something rotten wearing perfume. A deception. A mask.

My skin prickles. My chest tightens. The air shifts. Not outside me. Around me.

I reach for the small silver cross on my bedside. My hand trembles as I hold it close.

My voice cracks through the stillness as I whisper:

"Deliver me from evil, O God; protect me from those who rise up against me. Deliver me from evildoers and save me from bloodthirsty men." — Psalm 59:1–2

The words steady my breath. The air seems to fight back — resisting the prayer.

First, a tremor passes through the room — a tiny vibration, like something unseen is shaking against the floorboards.

My mirror quivers on the wall. The bulb in the corner flickers once… twice…

Then everything is still again.

Tired, I rest my head against the wall, and gasp.

And just in case you're wondering how filthy they really are — here's your proof:

This was never just about lies, or control, or power.

They were darker than I imagined.

More wicked than your thoughts would dare go.

I thought the paperwork was the weapon. I thought the gaslighting was the plan.

But they had something far more sinister woven into this story.

Because this wasn't just manipulation.

It was spiritual warfare.

And like all dark wars, it didn't announce itself with thunder.

It crept in slowly, disguised as ordinary things.

It started with the mold.

A tiny black patch near the window — one I cleaned, scrubbed, even painted over. But it returned the next morning. Then again. And again.

Then it spread.

To the corners of the kitchen. The back of the fridge. The rim of the kettle I used every morning.

To my pillow.

To the base of my shower.

To my Bible — yes, even that. I found it damp one morning, pages curling, ink bleeding. The mold had crept across Psalm 91 like it was trying to eat the words themselves.

That was no coincidence.

That was witchcraft.

That narcissist — that man who tried to claim my name — when he saw he couldn't control me with lies; he turned to something older. Something dirtier.

He began to chant over my house.

He sent people to leave things — small powders at the doorstep, oils smeared on my doorknob. Once, I found a feather and a string tangled beneath my welcome mat. Another time, a strange liquid across the windowsill — sweet-smelling, sticky.

He was trying to curse me.

To turn my home into a trap.

To bring confusion. Fear. Despair.

But what he didn't understand — what he *never* understood — is that the house he tried to curse, I had already blessed.

Every wall had heard prayer.

Every floor had been walked on by angels.

Every room had been sealed by the name of Jesus.

His witchcraft may have slithered through the cracks, but it burned on contact with the light I carried.

Because his chanting couldn't silence scripture. His curses couldn't touch the covenant.

He tried to break my spirit — but how do you break someone already broken and rebuilt by God?

So when the mold returned again, and the lights flickered, and the air turned foul — I didn't flinch.

I just lifted my voice and declared:

"No weapon formed against me shall prosper, and every tongue that rises against me in judgment, I shall condemn. This is the heritage of the servants of the Lord." — Isaiah 54:17

And like that — the power of it all cracked.

Yes, the house still creaked. The mold still came. But I was no longer afraid of the war.

Because I had already won it in the spirit.

What I didn't know, though... was that the next battle wouldn't be fought in these walls.

The enemy never stops at one soul.

When he fails to bring you down, he turns to your blood.

And that's exactly what happened next.

Chapter 6 – An Attack on Blood

I still remember the life before the darkness. Before the mold, before the lies, before the nights that refused to end.

Back then, the sun had warmth, not warnings. I was just another woman — happy, alive, surrounded by my family.

My sister's laughter filled the kitchen. My brother's voice echoed through the yard. My son — my only child — was my light, my reason to keep breathing.

There was peace.

Real peace.

But peace never lasts when evil sets its eyes on you.

His shadow — Adam Carter's — began to stretch farther than my house. At first, he came for me. But when he couldn't destroy me, he looked elsewhere.

Remember the man in the black jacket. He wasn't new here. He'd been there before —parked across the road,

Always watching.

Always waiting.

That night, he returned.

Same black jacket. Same silent stare.

But this time, the word *KILL* was painted across his back in bold white letters.

He sat outside my window, engine growling low, like a warning that death had been sent and was waiting for permission to enter.

I prayed — louder than my fear, stronger than his weapon.

I called on the blood of Jesus to cover me, and the Lord made the man leave. Not by my power — but by His.

Because every time they sent destruction, Heaven sent defense.

They tried again — more than once. Men at the corner. Whispers near my gate.

And every time, something — someone — stopped them.

The Lord stood between me and their plans.

But when their hatred failed to take me, they turned to the ones I loved.

My family.

That's when the visions began.

After I woke from the coma, the Lord gave me a gift — not one I asked for, but one I needed. The power to see beyond the surface.

To see what was hidden.

To see what was coming.

One night, I saw it clearly — the narcissist man sitting with a group of women. His hands rested on a table, his mouth moving, but his eyes fixed on me. Then, in the vision, he came close — too close — his hands around my neck.

I rebuked him in the name of Jesus, and he vanished like smoke.

But the warning stayed.

The Lord showed me something else that night — something I could never forget.

The narcissist man plotting with those same people... planning to use my brother as a sacrifice. A blood offering for power. For money. For control.

The Lord spoke to me clearly:

"Pray now. Cancel it. Send it back to the sender."

And I did. I went into prayer like fire — rebuking every curse, every scheme, every dark design spoken in my name or in my brother's. I called down protection on him, on my bloodline, on every person they marked.

That day was April 28th.

The very day they planned to take him. And by the grace of God, they failed.

The Lord turned their plans back on them. The same pit they dug for me, they fell into themselves.
Because what the enemy sends against God's chosen returns sevenfold.

But even as I rejoiced that my brother was spared, I knew this war wasn't over. The attacks would keep coming. The darkness would keep circling. And now, it wasn't only after me.

It was after my blood.

But the enemy doesn't stop just because you pray. No—he retreats, regroups, and returns with sharper weapons.

And this time…He went straight for the blood.

It began subtly. My brother started to look… tired. A different kind of tired—not the kind you sleep off.

He stopped picking up calls. Said he was "fine." But I knew something wasn't right.

Then came the headaches. The weakness. The weight loss.

And then — the diagnosis.

Cancer.

It came out of nowhere. No warning. No medical history.

One day, he was laughing with his friends. The next, he was in a hospital bed with a clipboard full of predictions and prescriptions.

But I didn't need the doctors to tell me what it was. I already knew.

This wasn't sickness. This was sabotage. A spiritual dart aimed at my bloodline.

Because the narcissist knew: if he couldn't break me, he could break what I loved. And my brother—my protector, my backbone—was an easy target in a war where no rules existed.

He wanted to **sacrifice my brother** — for money, for power — like the witch-workers who trade souls for their gain.

He wanted to offer my bloodline as payment for the darkness that fed him.

I went to God with my hands trembling. I remember standing in the corner of my room, pressing my forehead against the wall, tears streaming down as I said:

"Lord, not him. Please, not him. If they want blood—take mine. But spare him. He is innocent."

And the Lord answered me — not in words, but in signs.
The next morning, I woke with strength I hadn't known in months. My voice was different. My posture straightened.

The Spirit was upon me like a coat of armor.

I picked up the anointing oil and prayed over every doorway, every corner of the room.

I called out the names of every person who had plotted against my family and sent their curses back to the sender. I walked into my brother's hospital room days later and whispered Scripture over his bed:

"No weapon formed against you shall prosper."

"By His stripes, you are healed."

"The blood of Jesus speaks louder than any curse."

The doctors shook their heads. They said it looked "impossible."
But healing isn't their decision — it's God's.

And day by day, test by test, the tumor began to shrink.
Until one day, the doctors said: "It's gone."

They couldn't explain it. But I could.

Because they had planned a sacrifice, and my God brought resurrection.

But this was also my breaking point.

I had had enough.

There's only so much a person can take before something inside them stops trembling and starts to rise.

So I faced him.

Face to face.

The man who tried to rewrite my story and steal my name.

He stood there, smirking — like he always did — certain that the world would believe him over me.

But I wasn't shaking anymore. I wasn't the broken woman he thought I'd be.

I looked straight into his eyes — cold, dead, and full of pride — and I told him:

"You're trying so hard to rewrite my story, but you're struggling because this story only belongs to me. You're trying to kill me for my inheritance, but you can't, because I am a seed sent from God."

He laughed — a low, mocking sound — and I stepped closer.

"You walk around telling people you're married to me? I am not married to you, fool. How can you marry someone else in my name and say you're married to me? You never married me, and I would never marry a scumbag like you. You're saying you're me? You're not me. You can't be me. No matter how hard you try, you will never be me."

My voice didn't shake. His smile did.

"Keep following me. Keep stalking me. Keep coming outside my house, watching me, using my address for your selfish reasons — it doesn't matter. Every single thing you're doing, every attack you send — it's coming back to you. Time will catch up with you."

He flinched when I said that — the first sign of fear I'd ever seen in him.

"You're sending people after me to kill me? Sending gunmen to shoot me? I cancel that in Jesus' name and send it back to you a hundredfold. Everything you've sent for my destruction will return to your doorstep."

I took one more step forward. He didn't move.

"You want my life so badly that you're willing to kill for it? Then know this — it's going to be death before dishonor. If you ever come near me again, or send anyone to approach me, someone's going to die. Play your cards right before you approach me, because they're going to go down."

His face went pale. The arrogance fell away, and for a moment, he looked exactly as he was — small.

I turned my back on him. That was the last word he would ever get from me.

Behind me, he muttered something — a curse, maybe. But curses fall dead where blessings live.

And I am blessed.

He thought I was broken.

He thought I was afraid.

He thought the lies, the council, the witchcraft, the violence would silence me.

But the Lord had already told me — *No weapon formed against you shall prosper.*

And from that moment, something changed inside me.
No more fear.

No more doubt.

Only fire.

Because when a woman stops being afraid of death, there's nothing left in this world that can defeat her.

Chapter 7 – The Smear Campaign

"When they can't control you, they try to control how others see you. The smear campaign isn't about truth. It's about humiliation. It's about destruction without fingerprints."

After losing his power, after realizing his threats no longer pierced me, after looking into my eyes and seeing something he could no longer manipulate — he changed his weapon.

He traded whispers for broadcast. Lies for headlines.
He turned to the court of public opinion, and fed it poison with my name on it.

It began online. Subtle at first.

Posts appeared under fake names, claiming concern.
Twisted versions of my story, worded carefully to evoke sympathy — for him.

They painted him as the heartbroken husband, doing his best to support a wife "struggling with severe trauma and mental decline."

They called me "paranoid," "violent," "confused." Each post layered with the same message: "She's sick, but he still loves her."

It was a lie so elegantly wrapped in pity that strangers began to believe it.

And once they did, they spread it.

Comments flooded in.

People who didn't know me—never heard my voice—telling me to "get help," praising him for being "so patient with her condition."

What condition? The one he created?

The abuse became entertainment.

Then came something I could never have imagined—
a **movie**.

A production company announced a film "based on a true story."

Not mine.

His.

I saw the script summary. It read like fiction laced with fraud:

"A devoted husband fights to help his wife recover from memory loss, as she spirals deeper into delusion."

I wasn't consulted.
I wasn't informed.
They were filming in locations that looked like my street.
Casting actresses who wore my pain like a costume.

The worst part wasn't the lies they told. It was how convincingly the world received them.

Because by then, I had been buried under so many labels: unstable, unwell, bitter, broken.

To the public, I was no longer a person. I was a character in someone else's drama.

No one asked if I was okay. No one questioned why my voice was absent.

They didn't need to. The narrative was already written—and it sold better without the truth.

But I never stopped writing my version.

Because I still had something they hadn't taken.

My truth.

My name.

My story.

And no matter how many screens they fill with fiction,
there is only one real me.

And she's not finished yet.

Chapter 8 – Truth Restored

The bright rays of sun touched my face gently, waking me from a sleep that didn't steal my peace.

The night was gone.

The wind outside hummed like a prayer—soft, alive, untouched by lies. I rose slowly, walked to the window, and opened it. The breeze greeted me—cool, clean, kind.

And for the first time in a long time, it didn't carry the scent of decay, fear, or rot. It carried freedom.

A whisper in the air, as if heaven itself was reminding me:

"You are still standing."

I am **Allison Latoya Lewis**.

A voice that they tried to muffle, erase, destroy— not just by one man, but by a system that sharpened its knives with paperwork and polite voices.

They wanted to erase me from every space I ever existed in— my home, my name, my story.

And yes, that system was powerful. It swallowed women like me.

Women who didn't bend.

Women who remembered.

Women who said "no."

But see me now.

I survived.

And I'm not whispering anymore.

Because truth—real truth—doesn't need to beg for a stage or wait for applause. It doesn't require validation.
It stands, whether the world listens or not. It stands even when it's buried beneath signatures and diagnoses. It stands because it was never built by man.

It was written by **God.**

And when God authors your story, no human can redact it.

So yes—call me delusional. Call me angry. Call me unstable.

I will still stand here, in my truth.

And I will hand it to the world to judge. Because the truth is not for sale. It doesn't come with edits. And it doesn't crumble under scrutiny.

They made a villain out of me so they could justify what they did.

But I won't give them silence in return.

I give them my voice.

I give them every page they tried to steal.

And to every woman trapped in a similar war—

You are not invisible.

You are not crazy.

And you are not alone.

Because I am proof that a lie can stand on every rooftop and still fall. And truth, whispered through prayer, will still rise louder in the end.

Psalm 27:1–2 (NIV)

"The Lord is my light and my salvation—whom shall I fear? The Lord is the stronghold of my life—of whom shall I be afraid? When the wicked advance against me to devour me, it is my enemies and my foes who will stumble and fall."

Let this be known— **the narcissist man did not win.**

Because the God who walks with me doesn't lose battles.

Not even the ones fought in shadows.

THE END

www.ingramcontent.com/pod-product-compliance
Lightning Source LLC
Chambersburg PA
CBHW052116070526
44584CB00017B/2506